Amazing Animal Books for Young Readers

by Jean Hall

Mendon Cottage Books

JD-Biz Publishing

Read More Amazing Animal Books

Purchase at Amazon.com

Download Free Books!
http://MendonCottageBooks.com

Table of Contents

1. Introduction

Ladybugs seem to come and go without being noticed most of the time. They are cute and colorful insects. Insects are a living species that have a 3-part body, several eyes, 3 pairs of jointed legs and 1 pair of antennae. Antennae are long, thin sensors. Scientists that study insects are called entomologists. Entomology is a Greek word meaning segmented or cut into pieces. The study of insects is part of the field of biology which studies all living things. An insect's body has pieces that are joined together. Some animals have a long spine or backbone which means that they are made all in one piece. Insects are a diverse and fascinating form of life which accounts for more than two-thirds of all known organisms.

There are approximately 1.3 million named species of insects around the globe. Insect species are still being identified and classified, with a description and a name. Ladybugs have a smooth and delicate shell on the top of their body. Underneath, 6, tiny rough legs work together so that they can walk around. Watch them move, they are slow and steady. They can tip over by accident and they may get stuck. Their stubby legs and their round body will struggle to right themselves. Just give them a little push and they will have their shell back on top. When ladybugs cluster on a sunny, kitchen window they can be a pest. But they are helpful creatures in the garden, field and forest. They naturally feed on the harmful insects that destroy plants, crops and trees. Ladybugs or lady beetles fly and cluster together.

2. What are ladybugs?

A ladybug is actually not a bug at all but a beetle. This type of beetle is a part of the "Coccinellidae" group which has thousands of insect species. This Latin term for the lady beetle was used in Britain and it means little sphere. Ladybugs are called lady birds and lady beetles by entomologists. Most people without scientific training think of a ladybug as a round, bright red insect with black spots to decorate its outer shell. But ladybugs come in a wide range of colors and they may or may not have spots or markings. Ladybugs vary in size from .04 to .4 inches long, not much bigger than a pencil's eraser. They are round or oval in shape. Their life cycle takes approximately four weeks. Ladybugs begin as an egg, change to a larvae, evolve to a pupa and then finally mature into an adult. The tiny, yellow eggs hatch into a yellow or orange form with black markings called the pupa. The pupa will probably still be attached to the leaf or the surface where the original egg was laid. The pupa body will break down in stages of development and eventually the adult body will emerge from this sticky-looking coat.

Once an adult lady beetle is present in nature, it will live an average of 1 to 2 years. The tough, orange-shelled Asian lady beetle may live up to 3 years if the outdoor conditions are right. At first the adult's shell will be vulnerable, but with time the shell will harden. For unknown reasons, the shell's coloring will then become darker or more intense. Ladybugs mate in the spring and they leave their eggs outside to mature. Ladybug noises are silent to the human ear but they do make a slight, chattering sound that may be heard by some animals. When the chattering stops and the sun goes down, lady beetles go into a state that is similar to the sleep that we have. Some beetles may appear motionless and resting, while others may search about the garden and field for aphids or soft-bodied insects to snack on. Aphids are insects too and they are a kind of plant lice. When the sun comes up, lady beetles may fly around looking for their breakfast. Their tiny wings will make a huge effort to stay up in the air, and the wings will beat about 85 times per second. When they come to a stop and begin their meal, they will chew from side to side. When male and female "ladybugs" mate it means it is springtime.

The mating process brings several generations of ladybugs into the world during the spring and the summer months. Male and female ladybugs have 2 pairs of wings. The hard, colored wings protect softer, inner wings. The inner pair of wings allow the beetles to fly. On the top or the head of a ladybug are tiny jaws and claws that can grab their food. Just like furry possums, ladybugs have learned how to "play dead" when they are in danger since many predators won't eat something that doesn't move around. Ladybugs begin their life as an orange or yellow, football-shaped egg. Then these eggs turn into scary-looking, alligator-shaped larvae with black spines and bumps--yikes! But once they are adults, they assume the round and friendly shape that we all recognize.

3. Anatomy of a ladybug

The anatomy of a ladybug changes from its beginning as an egg to its final stage as a full-grown adult. The word anatomy means the parts or structure of a living thing. There are 8 separate and distinct parts to the ladybug's structure. Each part has its own appearance and reason for being. The 8 body parts are the head, pronotum, thorax, elytra, wings, antenna, eyes and legs. The beetles' head is flat and thin and it includes its mouth, antenna and eyes. The long, slim, hairlike antenna allows the ladybug to steer its way around the world as it senses objects to climb on or to avoid. These antenna can sense and feel more effectively than their eyes can see. Their 2 eyes, 1 on each side of their head, can make out dim or low light and dark objects. But they can't see the full range of light and detail that we enjoy. And lady beetles can't see colors at all. Behind the beetles' head and eyes is a structure called the pronotum that gives the head a round shape, a little like a smooth, partial helmet. This part of the ladybug's head helps to hide and protect it from bumps. And the head of a ladybug faces downward.

Below the head is the body of the beetle of course. The thorax and abdomen give the beetle its round shape and the wings and the legs are attached here. The thorax helps to join the head to the body. The body surrounds the bug's digestive system, the reproductive organs and the stinky, poisonous get that can bleed from its joints. The elytra is the shell coating or hard case that protects the sheer, delicate wings. The hard shell also keeps enemies from harming them. This shell is the surface where the color or markings are found. If you look at a ladybug closely (you might need a magnifying glass), one side mirrors the other with the brown, orange or yellow color, and then the pattern of spots. Ladybugs use their wings to fly around and seek the best feeding area. Ladybugs are awkward or clumsy as they fly. They might fly a bit right or to the left of the mark when they travel in the air. When they are done flying and bumping around, they tuck their wings inside the elytra shell.

4. Ladybug romance

Once the ladybug has found a good spot to rest her tired wings and feet, what happens then? We all need a little romance in our lives eventually and the ladybug is no exception. When the time is right in the early springtime, male and female "ladybugs" get together. The female hatches dozens or even hundreds of tiny, yellow eggs that are deposited under a leaf or near a tree trunk. Some of the eggs may not survive. Nature has planned for this situation and some of the eggs that do not hatch will provide ready food for the eggs that do survive. Most eggs need just enough time to hatch into larvae, usually about 3-6 days. If there is not an nearby food source, the female beetle may also reabsorb her eggs rather than laying them down in an area where survival is uncertain. Just like humans, there are different stages of life and development. For the lady beetle, the larvae stage is quite different from the mature beetle. From the larvae stage the beetles change into the pupa stage where there doesn't seem to be any progress in growth. But the pupa still needs to feed. The pupa form of the changing ladybug has a soft, bulky shape. All four stages are necessary in their own way and the final result is the adult ladybug. Then the life cycle repeats itself over and over again.

5. How to spot different types of ladybugs

Adult ladybugs do get around and they can be spotted in the sunny garden, scaling a blade of grass, or perched on a wildflower. They can have shells with gray, white, green, brown or even orange coloring. These colors may be solid with little to no spots. Or, just to keep us guessing, these pretty beetles can have black bodies with colored spots. The less common, destructive ladybugs are brown and hairy.

Females and males look very much alike. But females are generally larger than males. The color and markings on their shell protect them from birds who believe that they would not be tasty to eat. Types of ladybugs include: 2-spotted, 13-spotted, eye-spotted, pine lady beetle,

6-spotted oval convergent which has a red shell and black markings, plain red Californian, multi-colored orange spotted Asian, and the 7-spotted European lady beetle which has the classic, fire engine red shell with black spots. Look for the overall shell color and then see if there are any markings. Markings or spots can be found on the shell/elytra or on the head covering/pronotum. Like many predators or hunters, ladybugs feed on insects smaller than themselves to survive. In times of scarcity, ladybugs will consume flower nectar and honeydew. Because they adapt well to their environment, there are almost 400 species of ladybugs found in North America. And there are a total of nearly 5,000 species found all over the globe. These lady beetles have their role to play in nature and they do it well.

6. Are ladybugs helpful?

The short answer is yes. Ladybugs are useful creatures who live outside most of the time and they have a big appetite. They like to eat soft-bodied pests especially aphids which destroy farmer's crops. Aphids or plant lice, suck the life-sustaining sap out of plants. They have long wings and they are colored green, black or white. Aphid insects can destroy a tree or a shrub. You might see a plant that has brown edges or leaves that have wilted as a result of aphids. Many gardeners buy ladybugs to keep their plants healthy. You can even buy them in bulk and have them refrigerated for shipping purposes. Once you get them home they will perk up with a little warmth and a good drink of water. Besides feeding on smaller insects, ladybugs consume the larvae that can also devastate plants. These larvae can spread easily like wildfire. Larvae is a term that means the immature, wingless form of an insect. On earth day in 2013, 72,000 ladybugs were released inside the Minnesota's Mall of America to protect the shopping area's many tropical shrubs and decorative plants. This mass of beetles was released to be a natural solution to the problem instead of using chemical pesticides. The whole mall became a "food court" for the hungry beetle. Ladybugs need to survive themselves in order to feed and protect plants. Ladybugs can fly away from a predator or enemy but they also have a secret weapon inside their shells.

7. Why do ladybugs smell when they are crushed?

Ladybugs will ooze a sticky, foul-smelling, bitter liquid from their joints when they get crushed by accident or when they feel threatened. This yellowish liquid is a defensive weapon that makes them unappealing to enemies. When there is a risk to their life, ladybugs will squeeze out this liquid as if they are bleeding. Nature is very inventive and it finds a way to keep species alive, including small insects.

8. How to get rid of ladybugs

When ladybugs are not eating or trying to survive an enemy's attack, they will have a time of hibernation or rest in the cold months. Even the charming ladybug can become a pest if they wiggle their way into your home or into your apartment. In the 1990s many light-orange Asian lady beetles began infesting homes on a large scale. The autumn season naturally brings cooler weather and the adult beetles leave their outdoor sites to look for warm, protected places indoors. Sunny, Southwest corners of homes and other buildings, with their open nooks and crannies, can become an open door. Most swarms of adult beetles occur from September to November depending on the temperature. Ladybugs are attracted to the warmth and light of sunshine. They may decide to congregate on your kitchen or attic window, or doors with glass. Once they decide to make your home their own, they will sneak into crevices, baseboards, walls and attics. Light fixtures provide a good resting spot with warmth built-in. One ladybug may be a nice thing to see but a mass of insects needs to be taken away. Pest removal companies can handle large jobs but for most families, just vacuuming up the beetles will do the trick. Some may be crushed in the process, but some can be released back into nature, farther away from your home. Just use a paper towel to trap the beetles as you empty them from the vacuum canister. The adult beetles don't nest and leave eggs inside, so at least they don't multiply once they are in. This hibernation or resting phase is called "diapause." If they get enough warmth and light then they will stir around and get under foot.

Sweeping up the beetles is not easy because their shells are so smooth and slippery. Plus, if you smash the beetles in the sweeping process, the yellow liquid can stain floors and carpets. Blanket use of exterior pesticides may not help. It is a good idea to seal or close cracks in eaves, siding, windows, doors, and attic vents. That way there is no open door for beetles to march in. There may be no easy fix for the problem of a beetle invasion, but knowing where and when to prevent their entry is half of the battle.

Although a great quantity of ladybugs can be a pest or a downright problem, they will not do any physical harm to your home or to your apartment. They do not drill or bore holes in the walls or furniture. If you get the yellowish liquid on your hands, just don't touch your face or your eyes as it may be irritating. There may be a slight pinch if a beetle stings you but it won't really harm you. If the ladybugs are not being a pest or clogging up light fixtures, you can appreciate that they are small and cute. The charming image of this feminine-looking creature has often been used in advertising logos and pictures, especially the ladybugs with round, red shells and black spots.

9. How did the humble ladybug get her name?

This classic red ladybug with seven black spots is called "Coccinella septempunctata" by its Latin scientific name. The ladybug name has its roots in English history, culture and folklore. In the Middle Ages, English farmers may have prayed to the biblical Virgin Mary to bring the ladybug to save their crops. And the term ta refers to the 7 spots on the beetle's shell. The 7 spots may also refer to the 7 joys and the 7 sorrows of this admired lady. There were several famous paintings of the time that showed lady Mary with a bright, red cloak which caused her to be associated with the red shell of the ladybug. Other names for this beetle include God's cow, ladyclock, lady cow and lady fly. Because ladybugs are beneficial to farmers and they help communities to survive, they have positive names and a good reputation throughout history. It is generally thought that a ladybug is lucky and to kill a ladybug is unlucky. The famous Old English children's nursery rhyme refers to the ladybugs' role in the health of farmer's crops. Sometimes crops need to be partially burned off in order to stimulate growth underneath. And the ladybugs are there making their home in those fields and eating harmful insects. The rhyme goes like this, "Ladybug, ladybug, fly away home, Your house is on fire and your children are gone, All except one, And her name is Ann, And she hid under the baking pan...."

10. Ladybugs in the farming field

In today's world, farmers still need to guard their crops against predators to grow a successful business and to provide the food necessary for all of us to survive. Ladybugs save farmers money since they can use less chemical pesticides to rid their vulnerable crops of aphids and other pests. Farmers may plant strips of non-crop plants such as flowers to attract ladybugs to nearby fields. Farmers may also consider planting their crops near friendly habitats for these helpful beetles. The word habitat means the place and nearby area where a living thing makes its home. Ladybugs fly over long distances during the growing season as they search for a warm spot and a good meal. They are the best natural predator for soybean aphids in the Northern

United States. An attractive, natural habitat within a few miles of soybean fields is the best way to keep ladybugs on the job. Multiple farms in rural areas may work together to plant areas of non-crop plants and flowers.

Over time, farmers have really put ladybugs to the test. In the 1880s, California citrus growers were faced with especially destructive pests. They released thousands of Australian ladybugs which saved large orchards full of lemon and orange trees. The process took almost two years but the benefit to the growers and the general public was truly valued. Because of this dramatic example in California, ladybugs have been regularly employed to help farmers and growers sustain crops since this time.

11. Ladybugs and tree diseases of the forest

Farmers and growers have the helpful ladybug to protect their crops but the health and maintenance of the natural forest is also protected by the lady beetle. The warm weather months are when most of us pay attention to the trees and to the forest in general. The green leaves or needles make a colorful curtain to frame the outdoor scene. There is a biological drama unfolding in the forest, and insects and tree diseases play a large role. There are thousands of insect species outdoors, finding their own way to survive.

Disease organisms have their way of latching on to trees and to their bark. Diseases that attack live trees may be found in the trees' fruits, buds, leaves or roots. These sites of attack may be expanded to the whole tree. Ladybugs may come to the trees' rescue by protecting the bark that in turn protects the interior of the tree. Ladybugs are well-known to prevent the spread of pine beetles which can destroy large areas of a beautiful forest.

12. Ladybugs around the globe and in your backyard

The forest, garden or field makes a good home for ladybugs. Whether you live in North America, South America, Asia, Europe or anywhere in-between, ladybugs are there. Virtually all continents (or the largest land masses) have ladybug populations. The lone exception is the remote, Southern continent of Antartica which is just too freezing and unwelcoming for most living creatures. If you like to look at or study ladybugs, make a welcoming place for them in the garden or in your backyard. Make sure that there is enough water on plant leaves and that pesticides are not being used with the leaves or flowers that you can reach.

You may want to collect a few lady beetles to look at more closely. The spring season is a good time to find ladybugs active in the garden or in the field. Use a small plastic container, old pill bottle or clear glass jar to gather the beetles or their changing larvae. Hold the container just below the beetle and nudge or tap it so it can fall inside. If they want to fly away, you can use an insect net to keep them in one place. If you swing the net around you may tear a few plant leaves. But just use those pieces of leaves to place in your jar. That way the beetle has something to hold on to and you may be able to notice their shell's color and markings a bit better.

If you would like to see more ladybugs in your backyard or in your neck of the woods, then maybe you would like to make a small house for them to live in. This could be a simple, wooden or coated, cardboard frame with small openings so that birds and other enemies can not get in. You can paint or cover the house with colors that ladybugs are attracted to including light blue, pink and yellow. Place the house near a water source like a puddle. Or place a shallow container like a jar lid or a styrofoam plate with water inside the house. You might add a few rocks or leaves to weigh down the water source and leave a few bits of cheese. You can even spray the house and area with a fruity perfume to draw in the cute beetles. Go to the garden store and pick out a few trays of flowers and small plants to grow near their small home. This way, they will have some smaller insects just waiting there for the beetle's next meal.

And feel free to ask your family or friends that garden what plants grow well in your area and attract insects smaller than ladybugs. Other than aphids, ladybugs like to eat: Tomato hornworms, cabbage moths, pollen, mildew, mealybugs, scales, mites, bollworms, broccoli worms and whiteflies. Moths are flying insects that are active during the night. Pollen is the yellowish-green film that you see in the air and in the garden in the springtime that helps plants to grow. Mildew is a fungus that comes from moisture. Mites are pinpoint organisms that grow into insects. And worms wiggle around before they go into the dirt. Try to spot or identify different types of lady beetles in your backyard habitat. There are still many scientists or entomologists studying and finding new and varied kinds of ladybugs. The beetles can be found in your backyard slowly moving or gliding on the top of a wide, green leaf. Or they may appear to be doing a circus trick by walking or hanging upside down on a bent stem of a plant. Each kind of ladybug may behave differently, just like people in varied cultures, places and countries. We can only know and understand living things by comparing them to something that we have seen before.

13. Seasons for ladybugs

People respond to the changing seasons just like insects do. People are more likely to stay indoors in the winter when the air is too cold for their skin or the road is too icy for their cars to drive on. The spring and the summer will bring people outdoors to enjoy the sunshine, warm air or the water in the lake. In the fall with the leaves turning colors from light yellow, dark orange to dull brown, people may take a walk to feel a cool breeze on their face. Ladybugs become inactive in the winter and they find a warm spot to just relax. In the spring, they become active and they look for a mate. Then they can bring their eggs into the world. During the spring and summer, many ladybugs will travel toward a mountain area where there is the best chance for survival.

Their travel is a winding and awkward path, where the air currents and temperatures influence their direction and height. Once the temperature of the air reaches approximately 55 degrees, they may set down so that their round or oval bodies can warm up. The migration continues with snack breaks for nectars, flowers, petals or soft plants. When they have reached the desired elevation, hundreds or thousands of beetles will mass together to avoid enemies and increase their chances of finding a mate. The lady beetles will feed, and feed, and feed. They may consume as many as 22 aphids per day. In the warmer climates, the fall or autumn season may find ladybug populations still focused on surviving outdoors. And then the cycle starts over again from the beginning. The months pass and the seasons change.

14. Conclusion

In all but the coldest months, it pays for the ladybug to have a strong appetite and a bad smell. It is the way for them to survive. The life of an insect may be small in comparison to our large bodies and active minds. They have a pre-programmed way of living as only nature can explain. Masses of lady beetles can invade a home and they can be a pest for families. Or they can find their way into your garden and keep your plants and flowers healthy. Farmers and foresters rely on this insect to prevent crop and tree loss. When there aren't enough ladybugs in a field or a forest naturally, large populations may be released to bring the area back to full, flowering and growing health. So when you see a ladybug, what will you think? Will you think that they are cute or that they are lucky? Even if an insect is not something that you think about at all, the helpful ladybug is on the job and she is participating in nature's drama.

15. Photo credits

All Images Licensed by Fotolia.com and 123rf.com

Photo A. #7161489 Ladybug on the chamomiles, © Pavel Timofeev, 123rf.com.

Photo B. #8927983 Fresh morning dew and ladybird, ©Vaclav Volrab, 123rf.com.

Photo C. #47972460 Ladybug on a blade of grass, ©Ludmila Smite, fotolia.com.

Photo D. #140229 Close-up of a ladybug, ©Marek Kosmal, fotolia.com.

Photo E. #12595038 Macro of a ladybug larva, ©Christian Musat, 123rf.com.

Photo F. #351199769 Two ladybugs on a white background, ©Eric Isselee, fotolia.com

Photo G. #41074351 Orange-spotted beetle, ©jpbadger, fotolia.com.

Photo H. #3796280 Large, oval beetle, ©Ballunya, fotolia.com.

Photo I. #32260641 Bug in field, ©shima-risu, fotolia.com.

Photo J. #32425720 Black beetle, ©M.R. Swadzba, fotolia.com.

Photo K. #43388338 Ladybug on a thumb, ©mex99, fotolia.com.

Photo L. #6478531 Mass of ladybugs on a two-by-four, ©Catherine Murray, 123rf.com.

Photo M. #19580453 Ladybird feeds on aphids on a rose, ©Aleksandar Kitanovic, 123rf.com.

Photo N. #30725740 Beetle in plants, ©kogera, fotolia.com.

Photo O. #13643625 Red ladybug walking on a tree trunk, ©Ivonne Wierink, 123rf.com.

Photo P. #875803 A group of ladybirds take flight, ©James Thew, 123rf.com.

Photo Q. #11839786 Ladybugs swarm on the forest floor, ©Bill Sinkovich, 123rf.com.

Photo R. #4045623 Green plant growing through dead soil, ©nejron, 123rf.com.

Photo S. #40983552 Beetle on a flower, ©K.-U.H., fotolia.com.

Read More Amazing Animal Books

Purchase at Amazon.com
Website http://AmazingAnimalBooks.com

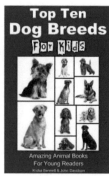

Top Ten Dog Breeds For Kids
Amazing Animal Books For Young Readers

German Shepherds
Dog Books for Kids
K. Bennett

Bulldogs
Dog Books for Kids
K. Bennett

Dachshund
Dog Books for Kids
K. Bennett

Poodles

Dog Books for Kids
K. Bennett

Labrador Retrievers

Dog Books for Kids
K. Bennett

Rottweilers
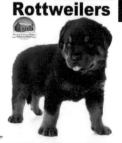
Dog Books for Kids
K. Bennett

Boxers

Dog Books for Kids
K. Bennett

Golden Retrievers

Dog Books for Kids
K. Bennett

Puppies
Dog Books For Kids

Amazing Animal Books
By John Davidson

Beagles

Dog Books for Kids
K. Bennett

Yorkshire Terriers

Dog Books for Kids
K. Bennett

Dogs
Top Ten Dog Breeds For Kids
Amazing Animal Books For Young Readers
Zahra Jazeel & John Davidson

Cats For Kids

Amazing Animal Books For Young Readers
K. Bennett & John Davidson

Foxes For Kids
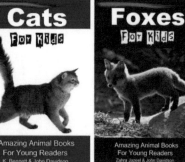
Amazing Animal Books For Young Readers
Zahra Jazeel & John Davidson

Wolves
For Kids
Amazing Animal Books For Young Readers
By John Davidson and Virginia Fidler

Our books are available at

1. Amazon.com

2. Barnes and Noble

3. Itunes

4. Kobo

5. Smashwords

6. Google Play Books

Download Free Books!
http://MendonCottageBooks.com

Publisher

JD-Biz Corp

P O Box 374

Mendon, Utah 84325

http://www.jd-biz.com/

Mendon Cottage Books
P O Box 374, Mendon Utah 84325

CPSIA information can be obtained
at www.ICGtesting.com
Printed in the USA
LVHW070312260320
651261LV00009B/473

* 9 7 8 1 5 1 7 3 4 9 6 9 1 *